Growing Old in a Turbulent World

A Collection of Indicators

Paul A. Strassmann

1

Published by Paul A. Strassmann .
New Canaan, CT 06840
e-mail: paul@strassmann.com

Produced in the United States of America

Paul A. Strassmann
 ISBN: 9798604379370

Growing Old in a Turbulent World

Personal View

Measure of Happiness

Country View

Global Perspective

Books by Paul A. Strassmann

Information Payoff: Transformation of Work in the Electronic Age 1985
The Business Value of Computers 1990
The Politics of Information Management 1994
Irreverent Dictionary of Information Politics 1995
The Squandered Computer 1997
Information Productivity 1999
Information Productivity Indicators of U.S. Industrial Corporations 2000
Revenues and Profits of Global Information Technology Suppliers2000
Governance of Information Management Principles & Concepts 2000
Assessment of Productivity, Technology and Knowledge Capital - 2000
The Digital Economy and Information Technology 2001
The Economics of Knowledge Capital: Analysis of European Firms – 2001
Defining and Measuring Information Productivity – 2004
Demographics of the U.S. Information Economy – 2004
The Economics of Outsourcing in the Information Economy - 2004
Paul's War - 2006
The Economics of Corporate Information Systems - 2007
Paul's Odyssey: America 1945-1985 - 2007
The Computers Nobody Wanted: My Years at Xerox - 2008
My March to Liberation - 2011
2012 Cyber Operations Reader - 2012
Outlook for Retired Seniors - 2015
Preservation of Investments for Retired Seniors - 2015
WWII Memoirs, 1938 to 1945 - 2017
Growing Old in a Turbulent World - 2020

Published Papers by Paul A. Strassmann

Harvard Business Review (1976) - 1 paper
Datamation Magazine (1976 to 1997) - 4 papers
Computerworld (1994 to 2004) - 115 papers
Knowledge Management Magazine (1999 to 2001) - 23 papers
Government Computer News (1998 to 2010) - 3 papers
Search Security (2000 to 2006) - 8 papers
Baseline Magazine (2004 to 2008) - 47 papers
Armed Forces Communications (2000 to 2016) - 39 papers
Information Economics Journal (2003 to 2004) - 5 papers
International Data Corporation (2013 to 2016) - 34 papers

Blogs - 381,461 viewers - (2000 to 2020) - 493 postings

Table of Contents

Introduction

There are now more than 630 million persons over the age of 65. Some of them are fortunate to reside in communities that could be demographically comparable to conditions in a "promised land" like Canaan.

The purpose of this review is to offer a perspective on the national as well as the international context of living in an increasingly turbulent world. Life may be peaceful in a particular location. But disturbances are encroaching on conditions everywhere because it is impossible to exist in isolation in a world that is interconnected.

This book offers updated briefs of easily read illustrations of the sustainability of prosperous family life as seen from an economic, social, environmental and security point of view.

The only known way how to make comparisons between the war-torn Europe of yesteryear and my current life is to resort to the already. published "happiness" measures. These can be tracked by separate predictors of conditions that could be associated with feeling of satisfaction with life. How our personal life will be affected influenced how the politics of the USA will impact our community.

The relative importance of local and country-wide influences is starting to fade as the impacts of a global society is starting to affect everyday life. What used to be events contained within national geographic boundaries is now influenced by universal technologies and by international trade.

My purpose is to write principally for seniors who are now enjoying their remaining years while seeking an improved understanding of their existence.

Paul A. Strassmann, March 2020

A Personal View

Town Median Income Rank

New Canaan ranks #5 in comparison with nearby towns.[1]

Weston	$219,868.00	#2
Westport	$181,360.00	#3
Wilton	$180,313.00	#4
New Canaan	$174,677.00	#5
Ridgefield	$151,399.00	#6
Woodbridge	$138,320.00	#7
Greenwich	$138,180.00	#8
Hartford	$ 33,841.00	#73

New Canaan, as a community, can be ranked by median income in comparison with other similar towns with have comparable population demographics in terms of age, race and religion. The #1 ranked community in this table, by median income, is not included as a small district.

Though these populations are comparable the actual differences with Weston and Greenwich are much larger than suggested by differences in median incomes. Such difference, such as between New Canaan and Hartford show enormous gaps.

The median incomes are not a sufficient indication of the disparity among the population in these towns since a substantial part of income of wealthy income comes from investment income that is taxed at a lower rate lower rate.

One cannot speak about the population of Connecticut as similar electorates. The large disparities within the State are caused by wealth and not demographics. For instance, Greenwich with a few billionaires, has also a large working class, low median income but untold pockets of richness.

---

[1]
htttps://www.google.com/search?q=Connecticut+town+ranked+by+income&oq=Connecticut+town+r anked+by+income&aqs=chrome..69i57j0.34855j1j7&sourceid=chrome&ie=UTF-8

Fairfield per Capita Income Rank

The population of New Canaan should be also compared with the rest of the U.S. Based on county per capita average incomes one can evaluate the New Canaan position on the top of per capita income. For instance, incomes for prosperous communities rank the Fairfield county.[2]

1	New York County	New York	$62,498	
2	Arlington	Virginia	$62,018	
3	Falls Church City	Virginia	$59,088	
4	Marin	California	$56,791	
5	Alexandria City	Virginia	$54,608	
6	Pitkin	Colorado	$51,814	
7	Los Alamos	New Mexico.	$51,044	
8	Fairfax County	Virginia	$50,532	
9	Hunterdon	New Jersey	$50,349	
10	Borden	Texas	$50,042	
11	Montgomery	Maryland.	$49,038	
12	Morris	New Jersey	$48,814	
#13	Fairfield	Connecticut	$48,721	#13
#3142	Wheeler	Georgia	$ 8,948	#3142

Fairfield per capita income will rank #13 out of #3,142 U.S. counties, ranging between the highest $62,498 for New York to the lowest $8,948 for Wheeler county in poor Georgia. That is an enormous range of 700%.

There is no question that on the per capita basis the Fairfield County is well one of the richest enclaves of wealth in the United States. Per capita income will not only reflect wage rates but also other income's which are primarily a reflection on how the wealth is distributed among the various counties.

Fairfield population has only 0.03% of the US population. Most of the U.S. population lives in counties below the average income.

2

https://www.google.com/search?q=Connecticut+town+ranked+by+income&oq=Connecticut+t
own+ranked+by+income&aqs=chrome..69i57j0.34855j1j7&sourceid=chrome&ie=UTF-8

Global GDP Rank

Ultimately what matters is the well-being position of the local conditions as seen from the standpoint of the global population. To rank that for the purposes of this report we can rely only on published international indicators.[3]

Country	2017 Average Income	% of New Canaan
New Canaan	$ 318,875	100.0%
Switzerland	$ 64,307	20.2%
United States	$ 51,485	16.1%
World	$ 8,826	2.8%
China	$ 6,568	2.1%
India	$ 1,678	0.5%

As an example, New Canaan 2017 average income was $318,895. That was a large number because it included at least one billionaire. In comparison Switzerland average income was $64,307, United States average income was $51,485. Country numbers are much smaller than the average income number for New Canaan because they are diluted on account of the large population that earns low wages.

The difference between New Canaan and Switzerland can be largely explained by the fact that the overall population of Switzerland includes a large number of working people.

The difference between the average income in a prosperous country in a prosperous county and the rest of the mankind are glaring. The global average income is only 2.7% of the income of people in New Canaan!

---

[3]

https://databank.worldbank.org/reports.aspx?source=2&series=SP.POP.0TO.ZS&country=WL

D#

World average income was $8,826, China $6,568 and India only $1,678. Such numbers are only a fraction of New Canaan because most of the world's population is extremely poor.

Migration of New Canaan Population

The population of New Canaan does not view the town as a permanent residence but as place for transition from youth through adulthood and then into retirement. An examination of distribution of the age of the population offers an indication how changes in occupancy are likely to take place.[4]

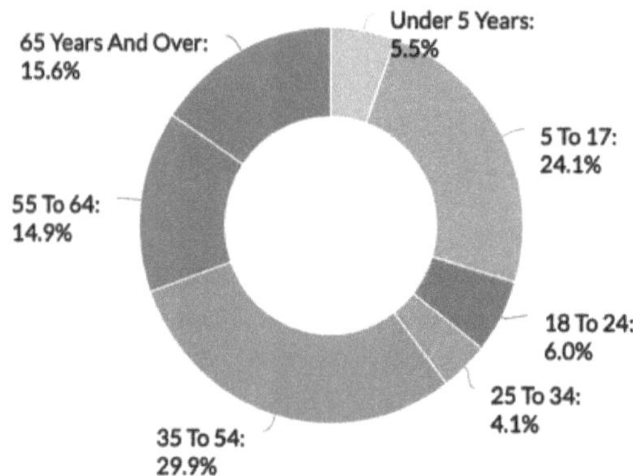

In New Canaan there are 9,128 working adults who are making 44.8% of the total population of 20,213. There are 15.6%, or 3,178 of senior citizen above the age of 65 who are expected to spend their remaining years in New Canaan.[5] Most of these people are retired or semi-retired. All of that indicates a continuation of a large amount of turnover in the possession of homes as well as the huge incomes realized by real estate brokers. New Canaan has a demographic problem! Even after accounting for the differences in a rising life expectancy due to improved medical conditions there will be only about

----

[4] https://www.neighborhoodscout.com/ct/new-canaan/demographics

[5] https://www.neighborhoodscout.com/ct/new-canaan/demographics

quarter of the New Canaan population that can be expected to remain New Canaan after the age of 65.

With a school population of 30% coming and leavings New Canaan every 18 years and 30% of the working population leaving time at the age of 65, one should consider this town as a transient community.

Distribution of Income in New Canaan

There is a diversity how incomes are distributed. The top 25% of residents have incomes exceeding $200,000 including millionaires. The bottom 25% of residents shave a fraction of this amount.6

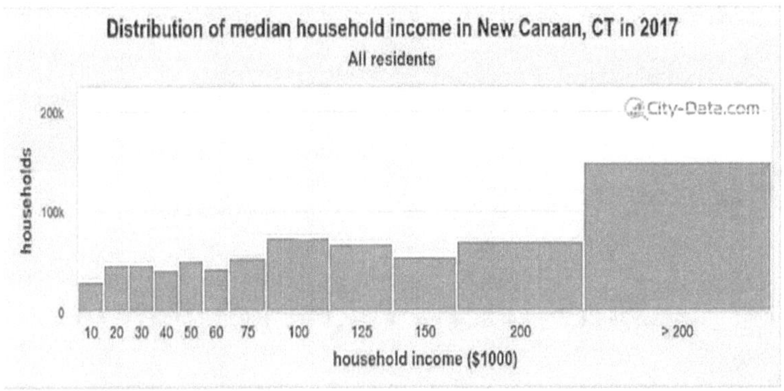

It is the difference in incomes that explains why the average incomes are smaller than median incomes. The much larger median income is generated by the many millionaires included in the top ranked 25%. A quarter of the population has incomes of less than $50,000. Another quarter has income of over $200,000 though there is no way of knowing how many multi-millionaires are included.

Local taxpayers are raised based on property valuations. Therefore, income or wealth does not enter into the determination how the tax burdens are imposed by local authorities.

6

https://www.google.com/search?q=Connecticut+town+ranked+by+income&oq=Connecticut+town+r

anked+by+income&aqs=chrome..69i57j0.34855j1j7&sourceid=chrome&ie=UTF-8

It is the wide disparity in household incomes that dictates how the community will operate with home ownership, schooling[7] and the disposition of accumulated wealth.

Differences in Wealth and Income

There is a great difference wealth and income are accounted for. The range in incomes between top and bottom earners shows smaller differences than the spread between the bottom ranking and top-ranking holders of wealth. The top 20% of wealth has accumulated 90% of all assets whereas the top 20% of incomes hold only 63% of all current incomes.[8]

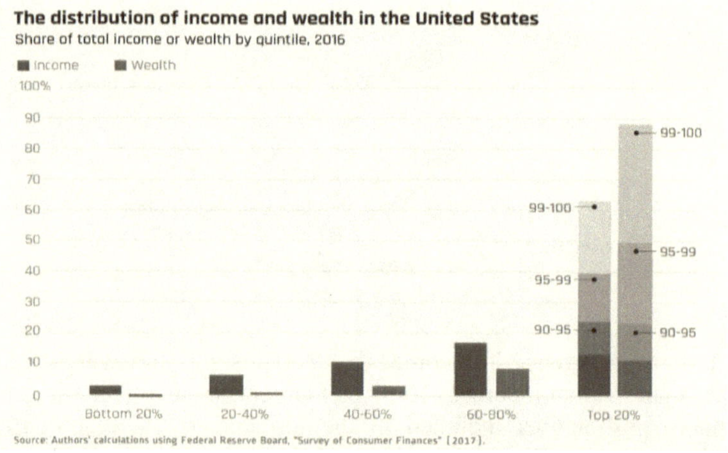

An understanding the differences between what is income and what is wealth is necessary for analyzing the distribution of New Canaan wealth. Such data is not available. The best we have are national indicators for income and wealth for 2017.

---

7 There are 4,241 students in local public schools, 1,347 students in private schools.

8 https://equitablegrowth.org/the-distribution-of-wealth-in-the-united-states-and-implications-for-a-net-worth-tax/

That shows that the remaining bottom 80% receive only 37% of all incomes and 10% of all wealth. It is the wealth of a few New Canaan households that shape how the town operates.

The wealthy spend only a minor part of their wealth in housing. From the standpoint of the allocation of social burdens the existing taxation, which is based on property valuation, is inadequate in assessing the how much the richest people support a distribution of tax burdens.

Poverty in New Canaan

Findings of wealth in New Canaan should include impoverished individuals. New Canaan reports poverty rates of 3.2% for town residents. It is noteworthy that the U.S. Census includes income of $12,784 as a definition for an "in poverty" person. In a town with a population of 19,738 that would add up to 631 individuals.[9]

Poverty rates in New Canaan, CT

Residents with income below the poverty level in 2017:
New Canaan: 3.2%
Whole state: 9.6%

New Canaan residents also include billionaires whose income and wealth totally overwhelm the contribution to the averages by the poor. How the "in poverty" people can manage in a town where the price of average homes is over a million dollars is hard to understand. There may be other means for overcoming the disparity between average family incomes and poverty levels.

We have been unable to identify how any measure of income or wealth correlates with happiness. Though New Canaan occupation frequently identify themselves as living in the "next station" to heaven. It is not clear that favorable dollar rankings by town, county or nation can be used as indication as to satisfaction with life.

---

[9] www.city-data.com/poverty/poverty-New-Canaan-Connecticut.

Although the poverty rate in new Canaan is extremely low at 3.2%, the State and national poverty ratios are substantially higher. When poverty rates are tabulated on an international scale the presence of poverty can range can exceed more than a half of the entire population.

For instance, Madagascar poverty rate is 78%, Mozambique 62% and Uzbekistan 62%. The World Bank surveys show that 736 million people live in poverty. 71 million of such people are refugees committed to hopeless lives.

Value of New Canaan Homes

Since 2016 there has been a reduction in home prices 22% according to the Zillow real estate services.[10]

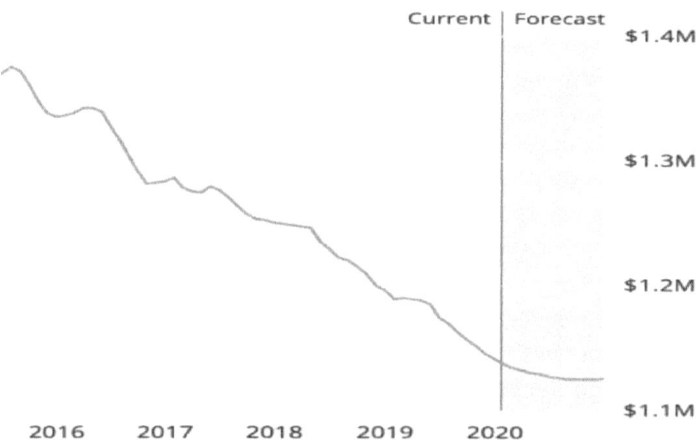

When a homeowner sells a house the estimated closing costs would deduct an additional 6% from the proceeds. For a highly mortgaged home there could be hardly any equity remaining.

The recent decline in the price of new Canaan homes can be perhaps best explained by the losses that took place when financial services personnel are now leaving town because the job opportunities have declined. The financial

---

[10] https://www.zillow.com/new-canaan-ct/home-values/

services people are most likely to have highly priced houses that show the largest percentage reductions between the listing price and what is actually realized as the sale price. Expensive homes in excess of $3 to $10 million are also heavily mortgaged because the owners preferred to keep cash in rising equities rather than tied up in homes.

Whether the shrinkage in the value of family residences can affect feelings of "happiness" for the inhabitants of New Canaan is not clear. So far only 3.6% of homes show a negative equity and 0.5% are delinquent in their mortgages. These should be considered signs that the large majority of New Canaan homeowners are not unhappy.

New Canaan Rain and Snow

There are appreciable differences in the climate effects on New Canaan from rain or snow according to a weather map provided by the National Weather Service.[11]

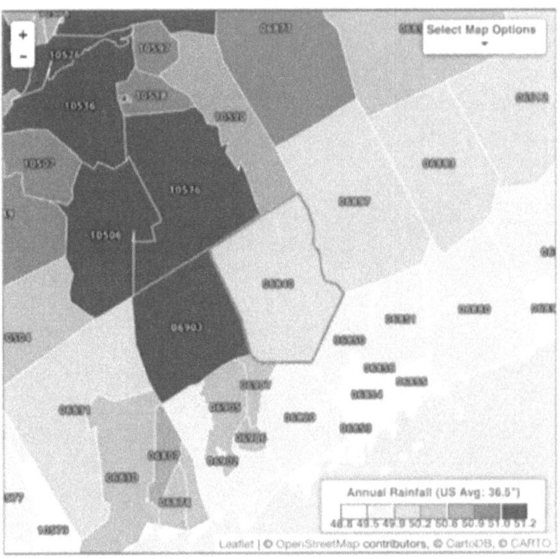

Bad weather, e.g. floods and snowfall, appear to bypass the narrow strip of land that borders the Long Island sound. In unlikely event of extreme

---

11 https://www.bestplaces.net/climate/zip-code/connecticut/new_canaan/06840

storms New Canaan is also well protected against sea waves by the Long Island to the south. There are also no known earthquakes.

Almost all of the land of New Canaan is at elevations of 200 ft above the sea level. The topography shows a persistent slope from high ground to the sea level, which offers protection against a deluge from extreme deluges.

Although the favorable weather that prevails in New Canaan is not advertised in promotional material it is nevertheless a factor to be considered in assessing how the population will receive such conditions.

Measures of Happiness

Happiness Rank Predictors

The following comes from the sixth World Happiness Report. Its central purpose was to survey measures the well-being of people. This report shows current rankings of the quality of life as evaluated on a global basis for seven "predictors".[12]

> ### *United Nations Happiness Ranking Predictors*
>
> 1. GDP per capita is in terms of Purchasing Power Parity (PPP).
>
> 2. Healthy life expectancy at birth.
>
> 3. Social support from Gallup World Poll.
>
> 4. Freedom to make life choices.
>
> 5. Generosity from Gallup World Poll.
>
> 6. Perceptions of corruption.
>
> 7. Measures for happiness, laughter, and enjoyment.

The World Happiness Report is a landmark survey of the state of global happiness that ranks 156 countries by how happy their citizens perceive themselves to be. The report is produced by the United Nations Sustainable Development Solutions Network.

The World Happiness Report was written by a group of independent experts acting in their personal capacities. Any views expressed in this report do not necessarily reflect the views of any organization, agency or program of the United Nations. They concentrate on rural-urban migration within countries has been are larger than international migration, and remains so, especially in the developing world. There has been, since the Neolithic agricultural revolution, a net movement of people from the countryside to the towns. In modern times it has hugely accelerated. The timing has differed in the various parts of the world, with the biggest movements linked to boosts in agricultural productivity combined with opportunities for employment elsewhere, most frequently in an urban setting. It has been a major engine of economic growth.

---

12 https://worldhappiness.report/

Rank in the Happiness Index

The World Happiness Report was first was released in April 2012 in support of a UN High level meeting on "Wellbeing and Happiness: Defining a New Economic Paradigm". It presents the available global data on national happiness and reviewed related evidence from the emerging science of happiness, showing that the quality of people's lives can be coherently, reliably, and validly assessed by a variety of subjective well-being measures, collectively referred to then and in subsequent reports as "happiness." Each report includes updated evaluations and a range of commissioned chapters on special topics digging deeper into the science of well-being, and on happiness in specific countries and regions.

Though the #19 ranked United States shows the third highest GDP per capita, it ranks lowest in healthy life expectancy and in corruption. The bottom rankings #156 is South Sudan, with abysmal ranking that are comparable with all other indicators for all African countries.[13]

The published happiness rankings are based on seven predictors of well-being. Dollar wealth, as measured in Purchasing Power parity accounts for only a portion of happiness. Health, social support and personal attitudes ultimately determine how people feel about their livelihood. That is why lower income Scandinavian countries will top the USA.

The World Happiness Report was written by a group of independent experts. Any views expressed in this report do not necessarily reflect the views of the United Nations. The published happiness rankings are based on seven predictors of well-being.

- Dollar wealth, as measured in Purchasing Power parity accounts for only a portion of happiness. Health, social support and personal attitudes ultimately determine how people feel about their livelihood. That is why lower income Scandinavian countries will top the USA.
- GDP per capita is defined in terms of Purchasing Power Parity (PPP) adjusted to constant international dollars, taken from the World Development Indicators (WDI) released by the World Bank in September 2017.
- Healthy life expectancy at birth are constructed based on data from the World Health Organization (WHO).

---

[13] https://worldhappiness.report/

Overall rank	Country or region	Score	GDP per capita	Social support	Healthy life expectancy	Freedom to make life choices	Generosity	Perceptions of corruption
1	Finland	7.769	1.340	1.587	0.986	0.596	0.153	0.393
2	Denmark	7.600	1.383	1.573	0.996	0.592	0.252	0.410
3	Norway	7.554	1.488	1.582	1.028	0.603	0.271	0.341
4	Iceland	7.494	1.380	1.624	1.026	0.591	0.354	0.118
5	Netherlands	7.488	1.396	1.522	0.999	0.557	0.322	0.298
6	Switzerland	7.480	1.452	1.526	1.052	0.572	0.263	0.343
7	Sweden	7.343	1.387	1.487	1.009	0.574	0.267	0.373
8	New Zealand	7.307	1.303	1.557	1.026	0.585	0.330	0.380
9	Canada	7.278	1.365	1.505	1.039	0.584	0.285	0.308
10	Austria	7.246	1.376	1.475	1.016	0.532	0.244	0.226
11	Australia	7.228	1.372	1.548	1.036	0.557	0.332	0.290
12	Costa Rica	7.167	1.034	1.441	0.963	0.558	0.144	0.093
13	Israel	7.139	1.276	1.455	1.029	0.371	0.261	0.082
14	Luxembourg	7.090	1.609	1.479	1.012	0.526	0.194	0.316
15	United Kingdom	7.054	1.333	1.538	0.996	0.450	0.348	0.278
16	Ireland	7.021	1.499	1.553	0.999	0.516	0.298	0.310
17	Germany	6.985	1.373	1.454	0.987	0.495	0.261	0.265
18	Belgium	6.923	1.356	1.504	0.986	0.473	0.160	0.210
19	United States of America	6.892	1.433	1.457	0.874	0.454	0.280	0.128

- Social support is the national average of to the estimated Gallup World Poll (GWP) question "If you were in trouble, do you have relatives or friends you can count on to help you whenever you need them, or not?" The GWP samples exceeded 100,000 subjects for each of the question. The primary researchers of every component of the "happiness" report are distinguished professors.

- Freedom to make life choices is the national average of responses to the question "Are you satisfied or dissatisfied with your freedom to choose what you do with your life?"

- Generosity is the national average of responses to the question "Have you donated money to a charity in the past month?".

- Perceptions of corruption are the average binary answers to two questions: "Is corruption widespread throughout the government or not?" and "Is corruption widespread within businesses or not?"

- Positive affect is defined as the average of measures for happiness, laughter, and enjoyment for years 2008 to 2012.

- Negative affect is defined as the average of measures for worry, sadness, and anger.

Governments set the institutional and policy framework in which individuals, businesses and governments themselves operate. The links between the government and happiness operate in both directions: what governments do affects happiness, and in turn the happiness of citizens in most countries determines what kind of governments they support. It is sometimes possible to trace these linkages in both directions.

The years since 2010 have not been good ones for happiness and well-being among Americans. Even as the United States economy improved after the end of the Great Recession in 2009, happiness among adults did not rebound to the higher levels of the 1990s, continuing a slow decline ongoing since at least 2000 in the General Social Survey. Happiness and life satisfaction among United States adolescents, which increased between 1991 and 2011, suddenly declined after 2012. This decline in happiness and mental health seems paradoxical. By most accounts, Americans should be happier now than ever. This is paradox: As the standard of living improves, so should happiness – but it has not.

Migration within and between countries has in general shifted people from less to more productive work, and from lower to higher incomes. In many cases the differences have been quite extreme. International migration has also saved many people from extremes of oppression and physical danger – some 10% of all international migrants are refugees, or 25 million people in total.

But what can be said about the happiness of international migrants after they have reached their destination? This report begins with its usual ranking and analysis of the levels and changes in the happiness of all residents, whether locally born or immigrants, based on samples of 1,000 per year, averaged for 2015-2017, for 156 countries surveyed by the Gallup World Poll.

The focus is then switched to international migration, separating out immigrants to permit ranking of the average life evaluations of immigrants for the 117 countries having more than 100 foreign-born respondents between 2005 and 2017. These foreign-born residents may include short-term guest workers, longer term immigrants, and serial migrants who shift their residency more often, at different stages of their upbringing, careers, and later live

Healthcare for an Aged Population

Out of total of 20,213 there were 15.6% aged over 65 years.[14]

Aged people have increasing demands for medical services.[15]

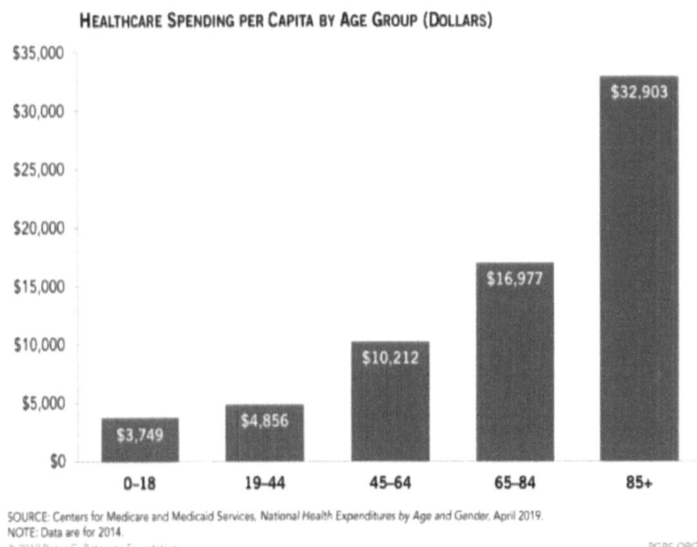

The escalation of healthcare spending beyond the age of 65 and 85 to $16,977 and $32,903 respectively is not affordable. The median 2012 income, from all sources, for a person aged over 65 was $19,604.[16]

Even after making an allowance for inflation such compensation would not suffice for the sustainment of food and housing needs.

---

14 https://www.point2homes.com/US/Neighborhood/CT/New-Canaan-Demographics.html

15 https://www.pgpf.org/chart-archive/0020_medical-spending-by-age

16 https://www.aarp.org/content/dam/aarp/research/public_policy_institute/econ_sec/2013/sources-of-income-for-older-americans-2012-fs-AARP-ppi-econ-sec.pdf

Health Expenditures as % of GDP and per Capita

The U.S. spends more money on healthcare than any other country.[17]

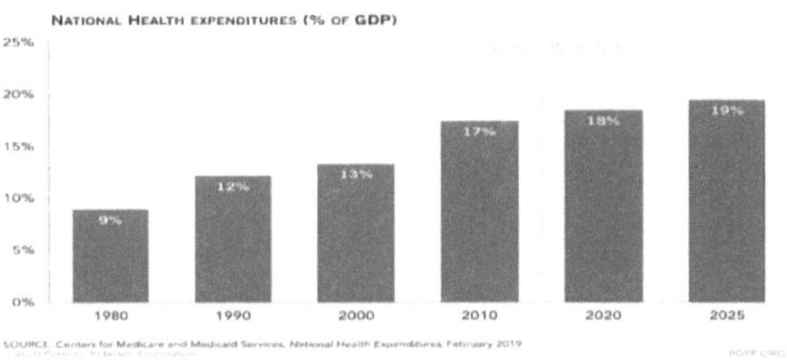

An international comparison will show that with per capita healthcare expenditures. The US spends a disproportional amount on health.[18]

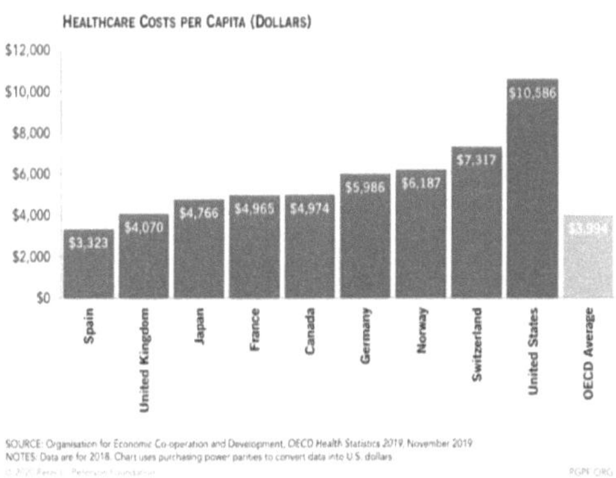

Such high costs exceed inflation and are less than the rise in average incomes.

The huge difference in the medical cost between United States and other countries is one of the reasons for the emigration of retirees

---

17 https://www.pgpf.org/sites/default/files/PGPF-Chart-Pack.pdf

18 https://www.pgpf.org/sites/default/files/PGPF-Chart-Pack.pdf

Healthcare Costs per Capita by Country

There is a wide range of healthcare costs, with the U.S. exceeding annual expenses by a wide margin. [19]

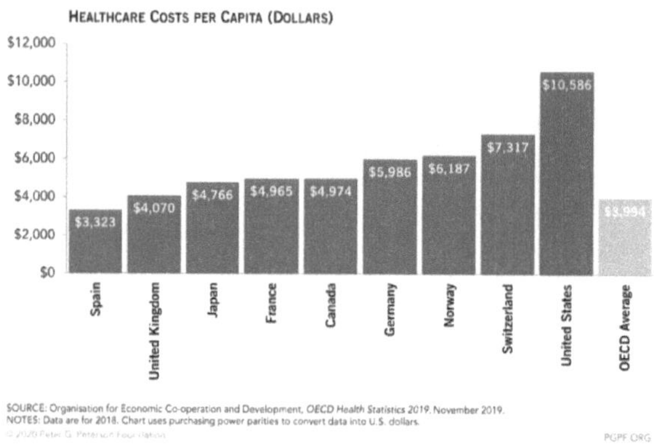

Even though U.S. healthcare costs are at a national maximum, the U.S. life expectancy is inferior. [20]

---

19 OECD Health Statistics

20 OECD Health Statistics

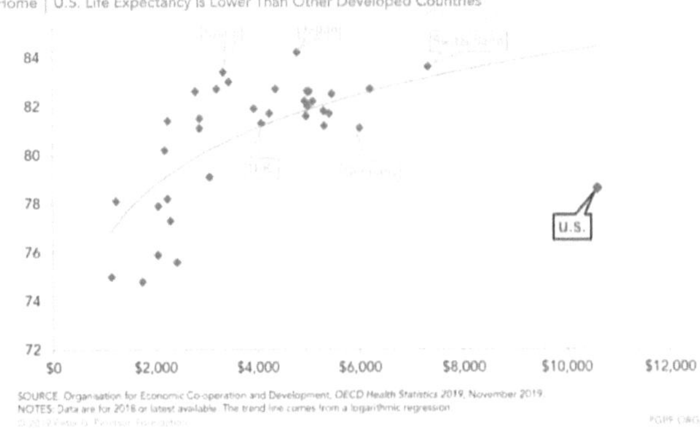

The US medical costs as well as life expectancy are clearly a statistical outlier.

Conditions from a Rise in the Aging Population

The U.S. aging population is growing creating increasing burdens to support the healthcare costs for the country.[21]

---

21 https://www.pgpf.org/sites/default/files/PGPF-Chart-Pack.pdf

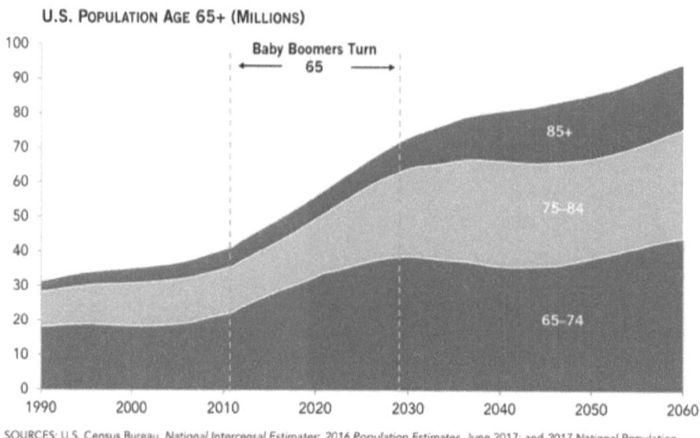

SOURCES: U.S. Census Bureau, *National Intercensal Estimates*; *2016 Population Estimates*, June 2017; and *2017 National Population Projections*, September 2018.

This situation is aggravated by the disappearance of funds that were presumed to support most of the social security and Medicare insurance payments.

The largest increase in the population aged 65 or more is taking place between 2010 and 2030. The increase from 40 million to 70 million shows gains in the number of retirees.

Retirees not only cost more for the economy but also place burdens on the social support system that has to provide for lack of income especially at the lower quintile of the income distribution. In Europe the ratio between the number of workers who generate social support taxes and the number of retirees is diminishing to small number.

Social Security Deficit

Social Security payments were supposed to be funded from a trust fund that collected the money from monthly payrolls. These funds were deposited in a U.S. Treasury trust fund, which was then used to back up bond obligations needed for the payment of government deficits. The net effect of these transactions is the prospect that the Trust Fund will have be depleted by 2035.[22]

---

22 Social Security Administration

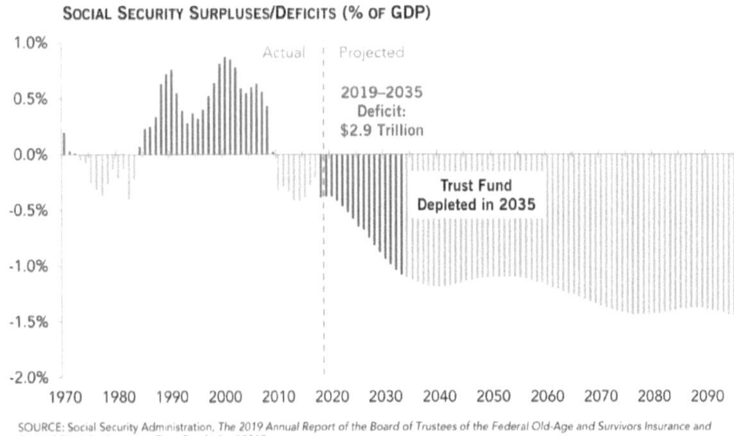

SOURCE: Social Security Administration, *The 2019 Annual Report of the Board of Trustees of the Federal Old-Age and Survivors Insurance and Federal Disability Insurance Trust Funds*, April 2019.

Meanwhile the social security funds will be run at a deficit of $2.9 Trillion from 2019 to 2035.

The prospects are that the payments for Social Security and Medicare will be reduced. There will be also an increase of the expectd retirement age from the current level of 65 to at least 70.

So far, such solutions have been proposed by a number of European nations but have been rejected by the workforce that has resisted the possibility of extending employed work life.

Skills that could be held by an employee over a lifetime are evaporate as technology is progressing at a very fast rate and the skills that are used to last do not hold up for people over 65.

Country Analysis

Total Accumulation of Wealth

The United States is by far the wealthiest country on the globe as measured in terms of its total assets, which includes ownership of equities, real estate assets and bonds minus debt. Since 1950 the US has added tangible wealth of over $100 Trillion. [23]

The growth in US wealth has varied since year 2000 as compared with smooth growth before that date. The most pronounced deviation from a prior smooth trend has been the recession in 2007 when past gradual gains have shown a sharp drop of over 50%. The incidence of recession is shown on the picture below.

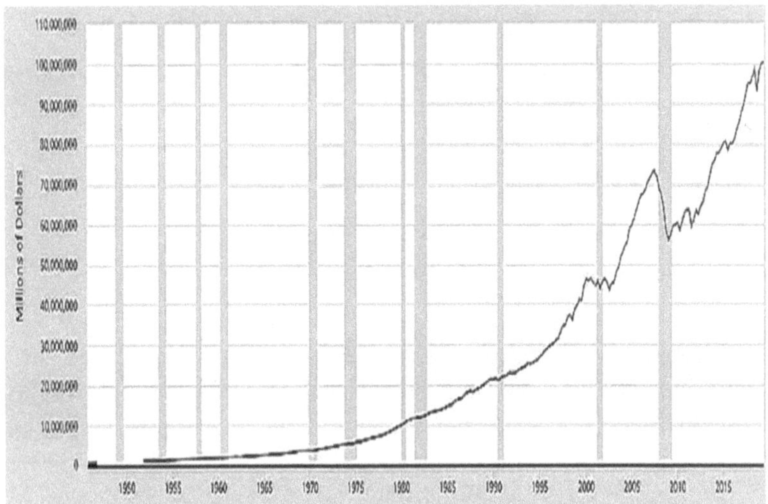

The question at this point of time is to guess how long the current steep growth will continue. Based on the former frequency of recessions such an occurrence may re-appear soon. The recent growth in US wealth has been accelerating. The key question now is whether US wealth in the future will match exceed the past after adjustments for inflation.

Notes where is he is the recession in 2007 were there has been a precipitous decline in the steady growth that has progressed since 1945.

---

[23] https://fred.stlouisfed.org/series/BOGZ1FL892090005Q

Distribution of U.S. Wealth

The large accumulation of U.S. wealth has its origins in the possession of 52% of the total aggregate household income by the 20% of the highest earning families. The top 5% of these family reaped 23% of total income.[24]

The highest-earning 20% of families made more than half of all U.S. income in 2018

Share of U.S. aggregate household income, by income quintile

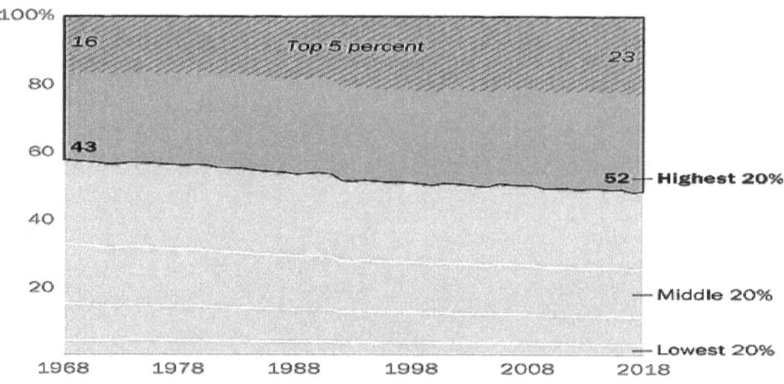

Note: Figures may not add to 100% due to rounding.
Source: U.S. Census Bureau, Income and Poverty in the U.S.: 2018, Table A-4.

PEW RESEARCH CENTER

The concentrated flow of cash to the upper 20, 5 and 1 percentile of the families created the available funds that enabled for further growth in investments.[25]

Share of Total U.S. Wealth of the Top 10%, 5% and 1%		
10%	5%	1%
77.1%	65.1%	38.6%

The top 1% of families share represents 1.3 million households in 2019. The distribution of wealth at the top 1% level has far-reaching implications on the ability of the economy to generate capital necessary for further growth.

---

[24] https://www.pewresearch.org/about/

[25] https://www.statista.com/statistics/183635/number-of-households-in-the-us/

Wealth and Inequality

Inequality can be measured either in terms of the share of total income or as a share of total wealth. They offer a different perspective on the sociology of the U.S. population.[26]

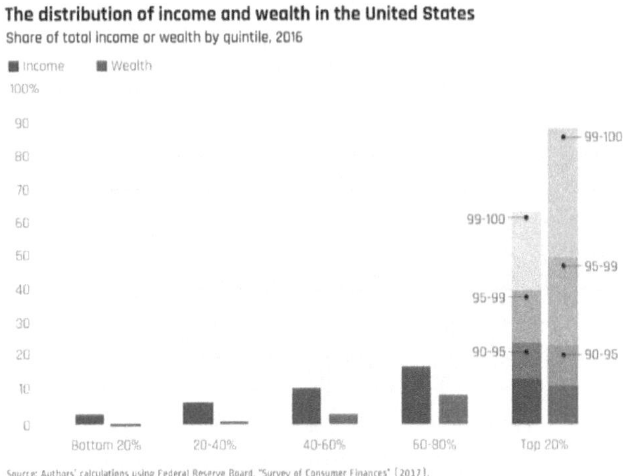

The bottom 80% of the population shows that incomes exceed wealth. It is only the top 20% quintile of people that shows wealth exceeding income.

The income of the top 20% will collect 63% of total income and an unbelievably high 93% of all wealth. The top quintile also shows even greater concentration by keeping the top 80% of all wealth concentrated in the hands of the top 10% and up to 90% of total wealth in the hands of the top 1%.

Weather such a high concentration of assets in the hands of the top 1% of the population is consistent with the needs to fund the capital investment for the 21st-century economy is questionable. Whether the holders of capital will make the necessary investments in new industries to replace the old capital that supported U.S. growth since 1945 is one of the key questions to be answered in the future.

The current propensity of the top 1% to invest in a future growth is questionable.

---

26 from Federal Reserve Board

The Sources of Wealth

The possession of wealth varies by levels of income.[27]

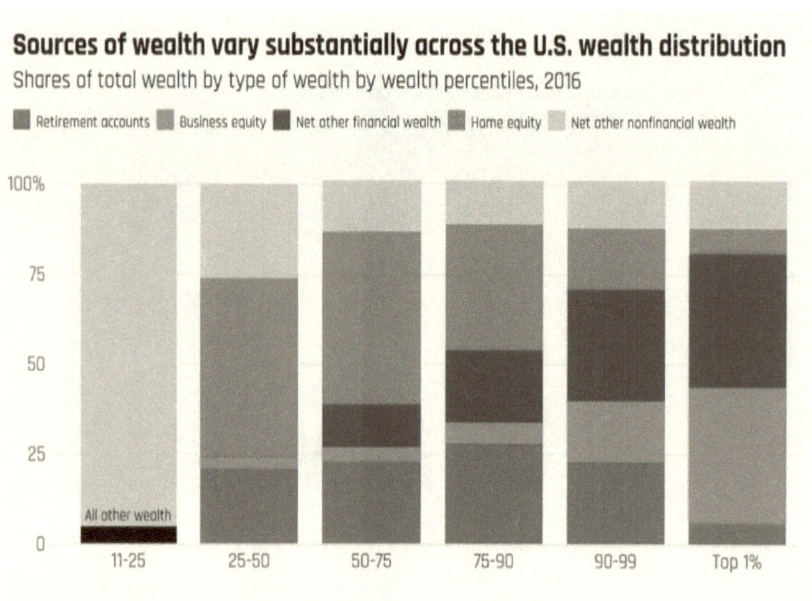

Source: Authors' calculations using Federal Reserve Board, "Survey of Consumer Finances" (2017)

The wealthiest 1% have allocated less than 10% of their wealth to retirement. They rely primarily on business equity and financial wealth to provide for their end of life, thus possessing substantial sums for making venture investments. Most of the venture capital and stock market prices are driven by the actions of the top 10% of U.S. families.

The wealth of the 25% to 50% of the population are families that have concentrated their holdings of wealth in home equity, hoping that an appreciation of homes in excess of mortgages will fund their retirement years.

It does not appear the least wealthy U.S. population, below the 25% group at the bottom, have investment-grade assets to dispose. They depend on public assistance for life support.

---

[27] from Federal Reserve Board

Is the Stock Market Overvalued?

Past stock market valuations are shown here exclusive of mortgages or market capitalization. From the standpoint of personal holding the tracking of the Wilshire total market valuation will therefore be more useful. From 1970 until 2014 the stock market tracked GDP, and then exceeding it. [28]

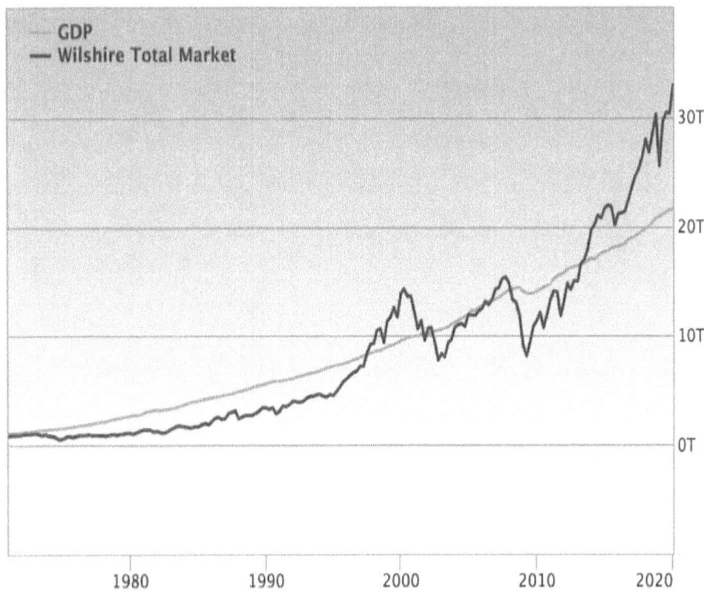

As pointed by Buffett the percentage of total market cap relative to the US GNP is "probably the best single measure of where valuations should stand at any given moment." Such advice should be now taken as the single most significant indicator in a state of the union assess assessment.

There is no question that the total stock market overvalued by at least $10 Trillion, as measured in comparison with the growth of the GNP prior to 1997. A restoration of market valuations to the historical trends would call for a short-term dramatic decrease in average stock prices during the forthcoming next recession. The stock market should not be used as a measure of growth capacity of the US economy.

---

28 https://www.credit-suisse.com/us/en.html

The Price-to-Earnings Trend is Negative

The excessive prices of equities relative to earnings have resulted in negative current returns. [29]

For the past 40 years there has been an escalation in the average prices of equities while the profitability of company earnings increased only moderately.

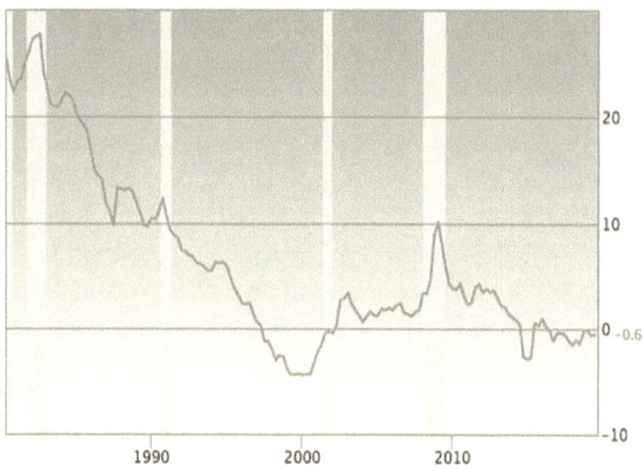

As result the prospects of shareholder gains has been restricted with the exception of huge profits that realized in funds that were invested by private equity and by mergers and acquisition. Employee pension funds suffered the greatest damage from failing profitability.

The negative trend of the price earnings ratio is one of the key indicators of where the US economy may go in the future. The current reversion of long term (e.g.10 years) and short term (e.g. 2%) at a telling indicator that the profitability of new investments will be negative (e.g. below 0%).

As the wealth of the top sector of the population increases its share of assets in equities becomes dependent on a parity of the ratio between profitability and earnings. Investor should regard this ratio as one of the key indicators to determine whether the stock market is healthy and not overheating.

---

[29] https://www.gurufocus.com/stock-market-valuations.php

Buying Power of the Dollar

The last twenty years have seen a deprecation of the dollar from inflation that has varied over a range of purchases.[30]

Category	Avg Inflation (%)	Total Inflation (%)	$1 in 2000 → 2020
Food and beverages	2.27	56.74	1.57
Housing	2.40	60.59	1.61
Apparel	−0.23	−4.48	0.96
Transportation	1.67	39.29	1.39
Medical care	3.47	97.78	1.98
Recreation	0.82	17.73	1.18
Education and communication	1.57	36.49	1.36

Medical care - with greatest impact on senior citizens - has almost doubled while the costs of apparel declined. Such differences explain the big differences between the monopolistic costs of local care and the highly competitive gains that were made from global trade with China.

Inflation represents the greatest threat to the well-being of a senior retired person. When cash is set aside for retirement the depreciation of the value of cash will have the greatest effect on the ability of a retiree to sustain an acceptable standard of living during extended retirement. That may require sustainment for at least 30 to 40 years of living.

The greatest cost of living namely health scare and housing represent the steepest rise. This may require for a retiree to relocate from well to do community to lesser communities where are the cost-of-living is more moderate.

Retirees may also seek investments with higher yields to compensate for the inflation. The adverse effects would be to increase risks and to expose the retiree to losses of accumulated savings.

---

[30] Bureau of Labor Statistics

Total Liabilities Exceed Total Assets

There is a rising disparity between U.S. liabilities and U.S. assets as result of a persistent policy to increase debt liabilities at an increasing rate as the perception of a rising prosperity favors deferral of obligations. [31]

A large share of the increases in US wealth have come from a precipitous increase in debt. At present the difference between the accounted book liabilities and book assets is $12 trillion and rising.

It is the rising spread between the liabilities and assets which constitutes the greatest threat to the financial viability of the United States and particularly to the value of the dollar currency. It is the widespread acceptance of the dollar as the global currency that supports the superiority of the performance of this country.

Threats to the valuation of the dollar, as the widely accepted means for conducting global transaction, is now rising in the form of an international

---

[31] US Bureau of Economic Analysis

digital currency that dispense with much the banking system supported by United States institutions.

Federal Spending and Revenues

The Federal government has operated at an increasing budget deficit.[32]

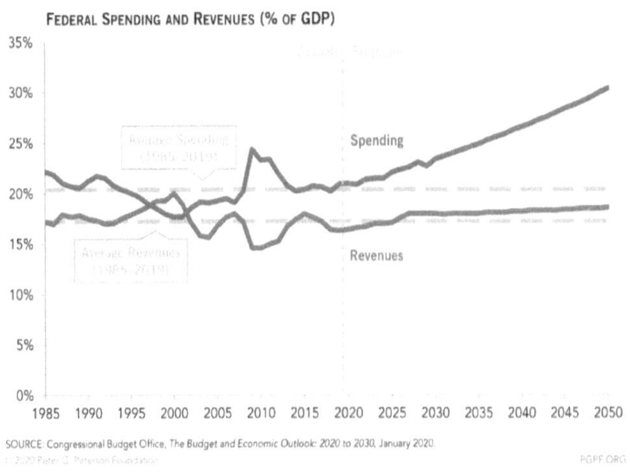

The dominant driver behind the spread between national assets in liabilities in the persistent deficit that shows it shows up as the annual Insurance of treasury knows from the federal reserve bank and that is then used to provide banks with added cash to compensate for the deficit.

Much of the rise in spending is due to additional money that is used to spend on new unfunded programs of the federal government. There are also cutes in the taxation that is received by the federal government to compensate for rising domestic programs.

Cuts in the taxation of Corporation who is perhaps the greatest effect on the rising federal deficit. The benefits of such cuts accrue mostly to people who are shareholders and investors where is tax revenues from the employed personnel is taxed as personal income taxes with minimal annual escalations. The spread between revenues and spending is now widening now amounts to over $1.5 Trillion per year.

---

[32] Congressional Budget Office

<u>Labor Force Declines and 65+ Population Increases</u>

The support of the entire economy depends on its labor force. Tax revenues decline when the labor force is reduced.[33]

A smaller labor force will now support a rising number of old people.[34]

The US population is essentially aging and in contrast who is the population in the rest of the world it is losing a large cadre of arising workers that would support which is economy.

Adverse demographics is working not only against the economic growth of the USA but also against an appreciation of wealth in Europe where at the birth rate has shrunk. Similar demographics of China will have a similar effect because China dictated to limit the growth in the population by restricting the number of children to only one per couple.

Immigration was seen in some countries as a source for overcoming the declining labor force. However, increasingly nationalist tendencies have now radically limited the importation of an unskilled labor force from underdeveloped lands to substitute or a declining labor force. The politics of

---

[33] Congressional Budget Office

[34] U.S. Census Bureau

extreme nationalism is opposed to immigrants on a racial. Conflicts are now being played out on an international scale with a resulting stalemate.

Share of Investments Held by Foreigners

U.S. investment holdings held by foreigners are an important consideration when considering the potential volatility of domestic assets. [35]

The net international position is now a $11 Trillion deficit and rising. That represents about half of the GDP and could be a significant influence the volatility of the stock market if international investors shift funds to foreign exchanges other than U.S. banks or U.S. equities. At this time that is an unlikely scenario because there are no comparable institutions anywhere in the world that can absorb the rising surpluses that are seeking a place where to invest capital. Most of the rise in US debt has been financed by placing debt with other countries that are purchasers of treasury bonds. This arrangement is a source of a potential failure if that escalates beyond the tolerance of the world to keep funding the prosperity of the United States. There will be a limit

---

[35] U.S. Bureau of Economic Analysis

where purchasers of treasury bonds will keep up with compensation of US for its rising budget and trade deficits.

In the years to come of what used to be kinetic warfare between the nations will increasingly find its form in conflicts about financial superiority. The strength of the dollar as a universal currency will be questioned.

High Cash Positions Held by an Investor

We follow the investment positions held by Warren Buffett, one of the largest U.S. private investors. [36]

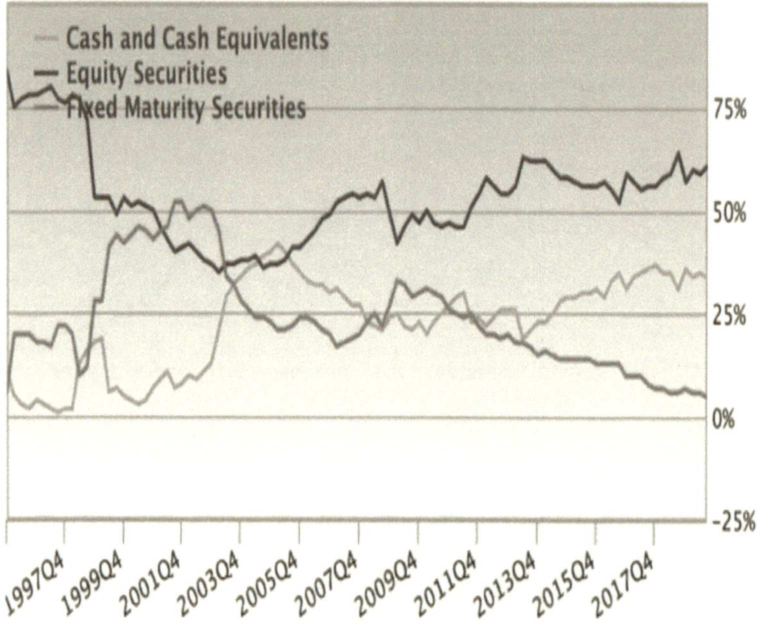

The Total Market Index is about $35 Trillion, which is about 160% of the last reported GDP. The US stock market is now positioned for an average annualized return of -3.3%, estimated from the historical valuations of the stock market. This includes the returns from the dividends, currently yielding at 1.7%.

---

[36] https://www.gurufocus.com/stock-market-valuations.php

As pointed by Warren Buffett the percentage of total market cap (TMC) relative to the US GNP is "probably the best single measure of where valuations stand at any given moment." Large holdings of cash are an indication that the current long-lasting market boom is coming to an end. Warren Buffett's cash position is in high yield funds while his equity holdings represents conservative long investments made on favorable terms.

Federal Budget Deficits Increase

Starting 2000 large federal budget deficit started increasing. There were no excessive huge deficits despite large expenditures to finance WWI and WWII. [37]

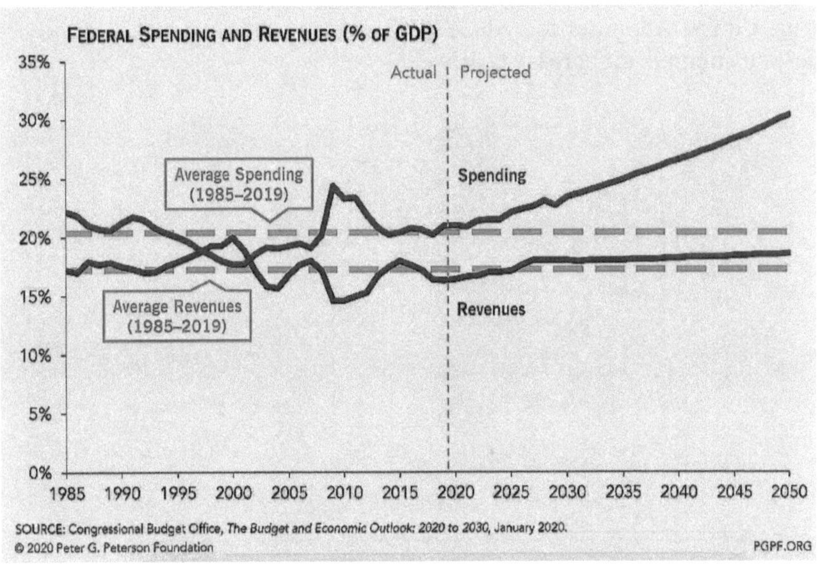

From 1905 until 1980 the Federal government always pursued the policy of funding expenditure with tax income. The extreme fluctuations in the budget deficit can be seen as a sign of decreasing confidence in the ability of Federal government to manage its affairs. A recent reduction in corporate taxes while increasing expenditures can be viewed as one of the causes in a reduced trust in the capacity to manage fiscal affairs.

---

[37] https://fred.stlouisfed.org/

A recent reduction in corporate taxes while increasing expenditures can be viewed as one of the causes in a reduced trust in the capacity to manage fiscal affairs.

The increases in military spending are insufficient to be offset by reduced welfare spending and for supporting a continuation of government enterprises.

Trade Deficits Rise

U.S. trade deficit is increasingly reflected in a rise of national debt. There was no trade deficit prior to 1985. [38]

The trade deficit increased largely result of a rise in the trade imbalance with China. Attempts to reduce such differences have not been successful despite attempts to increase tariffs.

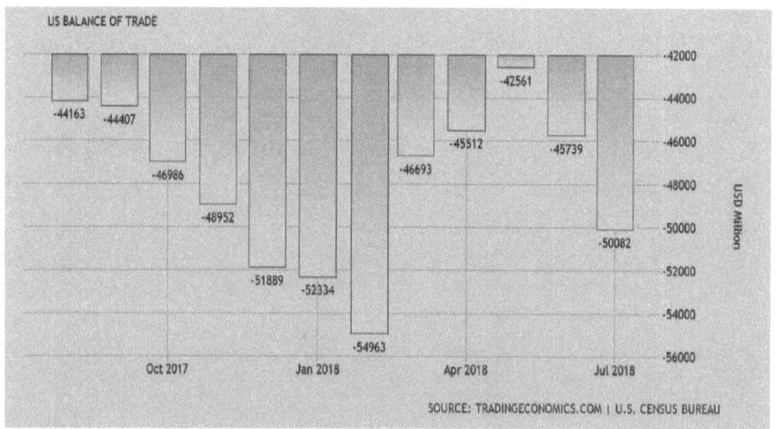

Such imbalance is unlikely to be remedied through increased tariffs but will require a realignment in the global value chain trading away from the U.S.

Trade in services has expanded faster than trade in goods. Distribution and financial services are the services most traded globally, each accounting for almost one-fifth of trade in services. The share of other services, such as

---

38 https://fred.stlouisfed.org/

education, health or environmental services, is rising rapidly, but currently accounts for a negligible proportion of overall trade in services.

The share of services in least developed countries remains small, although it has increased significantly since 2005. In developing economies, micro, small and medium-sized enterprises expanded rapidly as financial terms for conducting transactions became lover through the digitization of terms.

Lower Interest Rates May Indicate a Recession

The interest rate inversion – e.g. the difference between 10-year Treasury rate and 2-year Treasury rates has showed a consistent correlation with a coming recession. [39] The narrowing of the gap in interest rates, known as an interest "inversion" has been used as an indicator of an imminent recession in three similar prior cases.

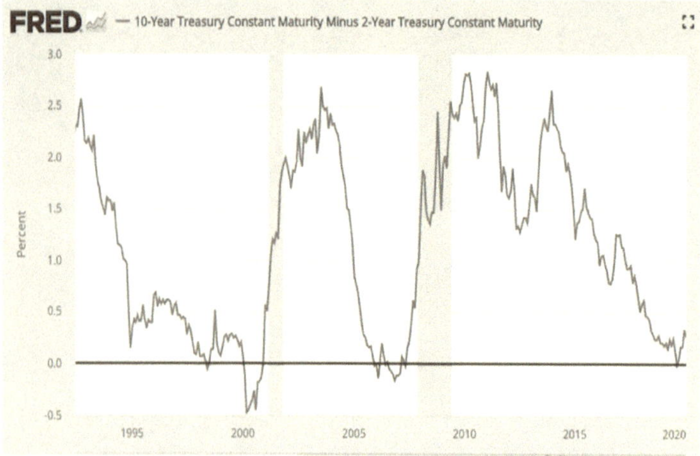

Will interest rate patters from the recessions in 2000 and 2007 be repeated? An inverted yield curve is when the yields on bonds with a shorter duration are higher than the yields on bonds that have a longer duration. It's an abnormal situation that often signals an impending recession. In a normal yield curve, the short-term bills yield less than the long-term bonds. Investors expect a lower return when their money is tied up for a shorter period. They require a higher yield to give them more return on a long-term investment.

When a yield curve inverts, it's because investors have little confidence in the near-term economy. They demand more yield for a short-term investment than for a long-term one. They perceive the near-term as riskier than the distant future. They would prefer to buy long-term bonds and tie up their money for years even though they receive lower yields. They would only do this if they think the economy is getting worse in the near-term.

---

39 https://fred.stlouisfed.org/

US Debt Has Risen by $13 Trillion

Since 2008 the debt has risen by 240% largely as result of recent budget and trade deficits. [40]

The rise in in US debt subsequent to the 2007 recession is considered as a significant sign in the deterioration of the financial strength of the dollar. The $13 Trillion in Federal debt rise now represents 62% of the nation's GDP, but only a fraction of other obligations.

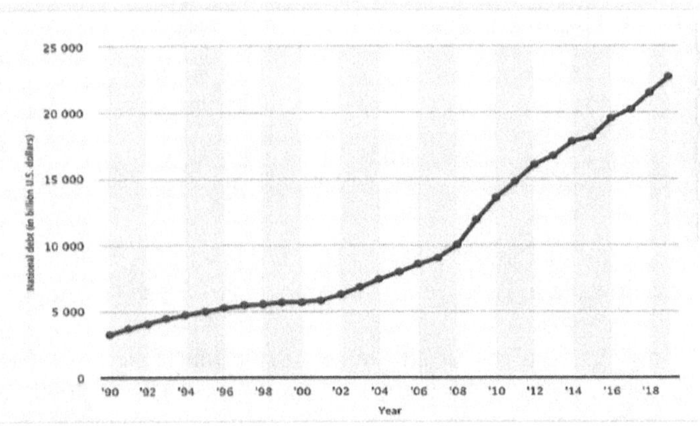

The steep rise in Federal debt since the recession in 2007 reflects the Congressional inclination to cover up deficits through printing fiat currency,

As represented in the statistic above, the public debt of the United States is continuously rising. Public debt, also known as national and governmental debt, is the debt owed by a nations' central government. A government debt is an indirect debt of the countries' taxpayers. The federal debt reached 103% of GDP in second quarter 2019. These numbers, however, don't properly reflect the amount owed by the federal government to *private* bondholders, since certain federal agencies (primarily, the Social Security trust funds) also hold federal debt. These agency bond holdings are liabilities the federal government owes to itself and therefore should be netted out.

---

40 https://www.statista.com/statistics/187867/public-debt-of-the-united-states-since-1990/

U.S. Household Nominal Debt

Debt that will have to be repaid from current budgets.[41]

2018 Nominal Debts	$ Billions
US Federal Debt	$21,407
US State Debt	$1,182
US Local Debt	$1,911
Mortgage debt	$15,134
Stock. Market Margin Debt	$655
Student Loan Debt	$1,544
Credit Card Debt	$1,039
US Total Debt	$42,872

Though the mortgage debt represents a third of nominal (e.g. recorded) debts it would have to be offset by the amounts of the remaining home equity.

In New Canaan 70% of all homes have a mortgage.[42] Outstanding U.S. mortgage debt rose to $15.8 trillion in the third quarter of 2019, according to the Federal Reserve. Combined home, farm, multifamily and commercial mortgage debt increased 1.2% from the prior period, the largest quarter-to-quarter gain in almost two years.

The biggest chunk of debt was held on homes, at $11.1 trillion, followed by commercial, with $3 trillion of loans, multifamily at $1.6 trillion and farms at $254.1 billion, according to the Fed data.

Mortgage debt is rising as U.S. real estate values gain. The value of all U.S. owner-occupied homes increased to a record $29.2 trillion in the third quarter, 21% higher than the bubble peak reached in 2006, according to the Fed. Low mortgage rates boost real estate prices, and hence the volume of loans, because cheaper financing means buyers qualify for higher-balance mortgages and can bid more for properties they want.

---

[41] https://www.usdebtclock.org/

[42] https://www.point2homes.com/US/Neighborhood/CT/New-Canaan-Demographics.html

U.S. Total Debt Plus Unfunded Obligations

In addition to the recorded debt, there are an estimate $75 Trillion of U.S. obligations for which reserve funding have not been as yet provided.[43]f

While funded debt is a long-term borrowing, unfunded debt is a short-term financial obligation that comes due in a year or less. Many companies that use short-term or unfunded debt are those that may be strapped for cash when there isn't enough revenue to cover routine expenses.

Unfunded loan commitments are those commitments made by a Financial institution that are contractual obligations for future funding. They should not be confused with Letters of credit which require certain trigger events before funding is needed. Increasingly, originating lending institutions are selling Senior loans and related funded or unfunded commitments to institutional investors like. Investment management firms, mutual funds and open revolving or open end credit is a type of loan (known informally as a Line of credit) allows the borrower to continue to borrow up to the original loan amount. Principal reductions are immediately available for future advances.

The largest contingent liabilities are the unfunded pension as well as veteran's life payments that have been obligated by legislation. Social Security and Medicare liabilities will become the greatest budgetary burdens as rising interest payments increase budgetary deficits.

---

[43] https://www.usdebtclock.org

A Global Perspective

Major Shifts in the Share of the World's GDP

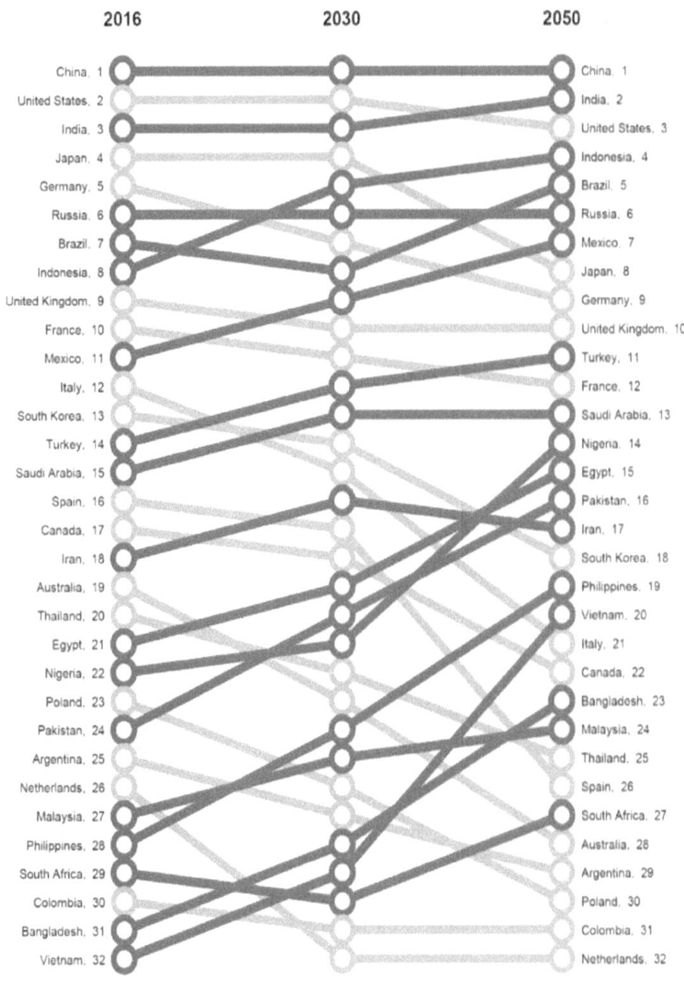

These shifts are dramatized by China's gains of 20% while the U.S. and Europe declined by 12% and 9%. [44]

---

44 https://www.pwc.com/

Increases and Decreases in the World's GDP

The ranking of the top global countries, arranged in order of their 2016, 2030 and 2050 years, portrays of the current best projection how economic power will shift from the U.S. to China and India as well as existing dominant European countries will yield to emerging nations. This compilation has been prepared by the consulting arm of Price Waterhouse, now a part of the IBM organization. [45]

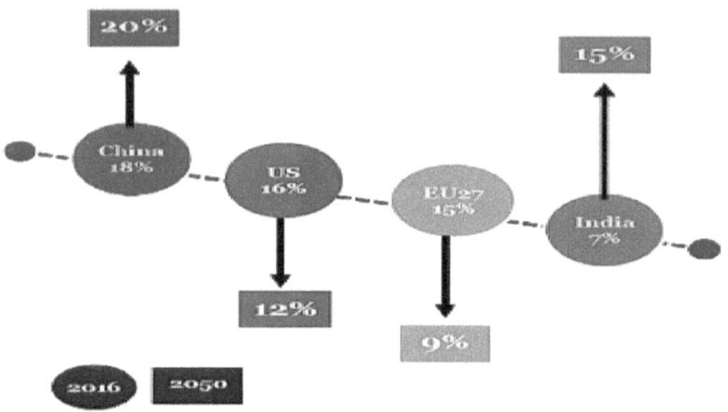

India is also gaining 15%.

Such shifts have far reaching implications on global trade. The U.S. and the EU, formerly with 31% of global GDP will have in 2050 only 21% of global GDP. That is a 32% reduction. Meanwhile China and India rise from 25% of global GDP to 35% of GDP, exceeding the U.S. and EU by 14%.

With China and India consumer consumption as well as infrastructure rising at a faster rate the global value chains for goods and services will adapt accordingly.

The question is whether the U.S. and EU will also shift their economies to fit the new conditions.

---

[45] https://www.pwc.com/

Total Market Capitalization and GDP of Countries

In terms of financial wealth U.S. shows the largest accumulation of assets.[46]

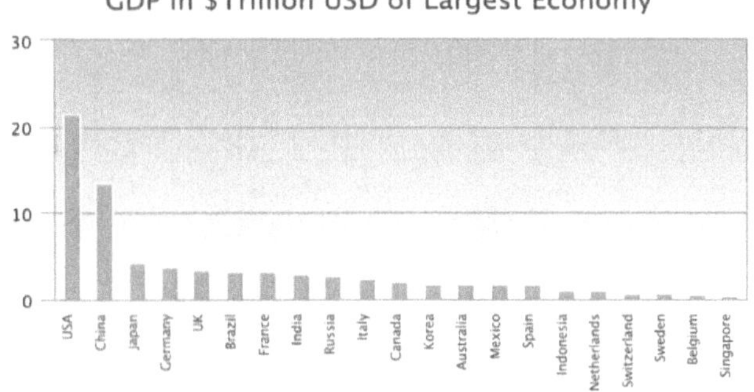

The current U.S. market capitalization on stock exchanges exceeds the combined capitalization of all other countries. This reflects the global distribution of GDP where only the rapidly growing China approaches the U.S.

It appears that China will be the largest gainer. India is so far negligible.

[46] https://www.gurufocus.com/global-market-valuation.php

<u>Current Average Investment Returns</u>

The global shifts in economic ranking other than in emerging countries are large the result of different investment returns ranging from 15% in Singapore to negative returns in the U.S. [47]

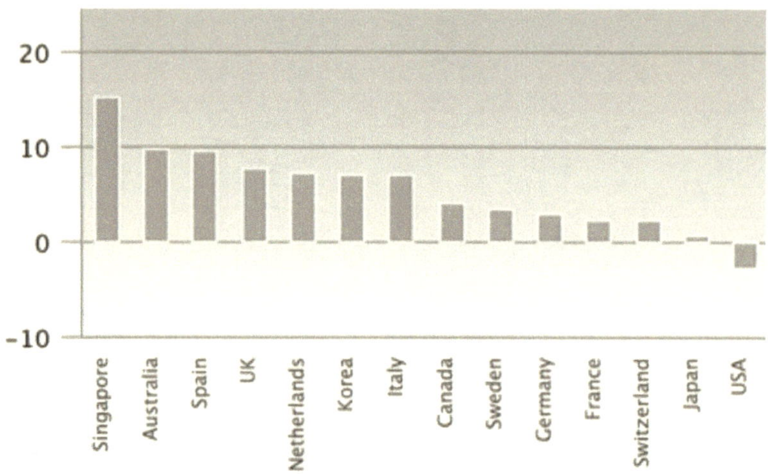

It is the negative investment returns in the U.S. that explain is decline in the global share in international trade. The major effect on investment returns is the extremely high valuation of U.S. shares. The Price/Earning ratio of the S&P 500 now exceeds the levels that were recorded only during the 1929 depression.

2019 investments come after the worst year for returns from global equities since the Global Financial Crisis with a decline of 9%. The accommodating monetary environment and conditions of low volatility that provided the comforting backdrop for the extended bull market conditions we have seen for a decade or so have reversed. The international confrontations over global trade have brought into focus a source of market and economic risk that few investors have had to contemplate before. Countries are now threatening trade wars are not where stock markets have fared the worst. A more tempered view is a natural consequence of what by historical standards remains a world of low real interest rates. To this point, in documenting the

---

47 https://www.gurufocus.com/global-market-valuation.pshp

long-run history of real interest rates in 23 countries since 1900. Future returns on equities and bonds will tend to be lower rather than higher.

Accounting for Shadow Funds

There are large funds that are not regulated by any government agency and that are not accounted in the banking system. That includes private equity money, illegal funds and cash that is used for criminal transactions or untraceable transactions - so called "shadow banking". Business in Africa, Latin America and the Mid-East is often handled in this way manner. [48]

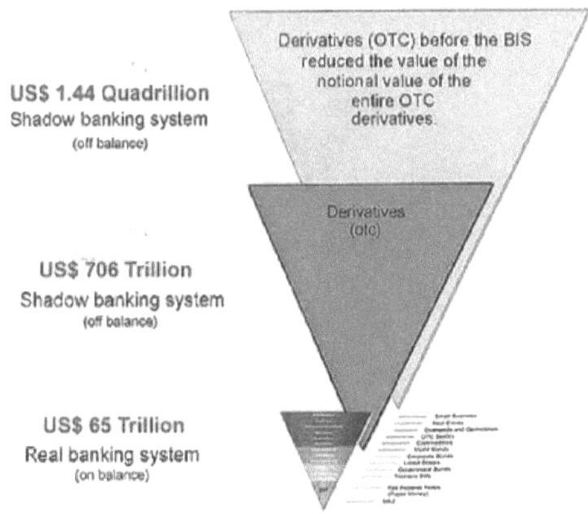

However, that largest funds are tied up in derivative contracts where investors commit money in insurance-like commitments to safeguard risky commitments by third party and particularly by speculators.

A derivative is a contract between two or more parties whose value is based on an agreed-upon underlying financial asset (like a security) or set of assets (like an index). Common underlying instruments include bonds, commodities, currencies, interest rates, market indexes, and stocks.

Derivative do not appear to be listed as a part of business transactions except when financial distress forces payments of previously assured assets. One of the primary causes of the collapse of the stock market in the 2007 was the in ability of the AIG company to meet its derivative commitments. A world's leading investor called derivatives to be "weapons of mass

---

48 https://topforeignstocks.com/2011/08/23/how-big-is-the-global-financial-industry/

destruction". Derivatives have become so huge because it is providing some economic value to their users under normal conditions. Derivatives were invented as insurance for the companies to separate and trade various kinds of risks.

Percentage of Global Millionaires

There are many millionaires in every country, but they are primarily concentrated in the U.S. [49]

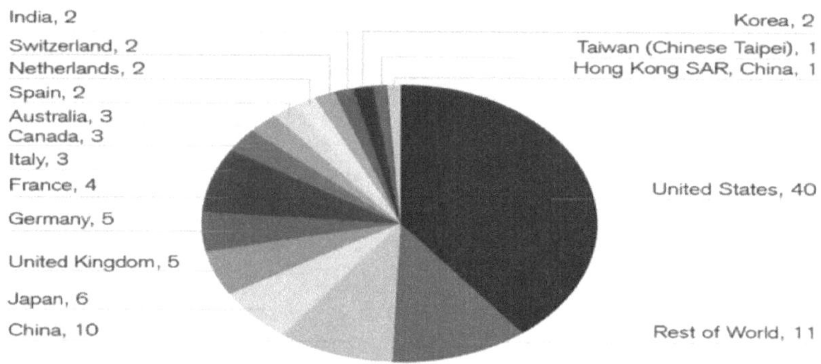

40% of the total of global millionaires are in the U.S. with the next largest number in China. Such comparison does not adequately reflect the fact that it is easier to become a billionaire in a poor country than in a poor economy.

It is the extreme concentration of wealth in the U.S. that explains how the economy functions. With over 90% of available funds available for investment it will be behavior of the millionaire class that will dictate how capital is used. With every incentive to use capital for realizing short-term returns, the multitude of millionaires will tend to maximize gains from ventures that can deliver only immediate gains.

Since 2008, average real USD wealth growth in Europe has been negative, in part due to the retrenchment of the euro. North America has taken the lead among the developed nation groupings, accounting for one-third of

---

[49] https://www.credit-suisse.com/about-us/en/reports-research.html

the rise in global wealth per adult. However, China has more than matched North America in the post-crisis era. Other emerging market economies have also made a significant contribution to real global growth since 2008. The net result is that emerging economies including China account for two-thirds of the real wealth gain since 2008 or double the contribution of North America.

Concentration of Millionaires

In the concentration of wealth what matters is not only the number of millionaires but also the accumulation of wealth they are holding. U.S. millionaires have the distinction of also holding the greatest accumulation of large wealth which in some cases makes them billionaires. [50]

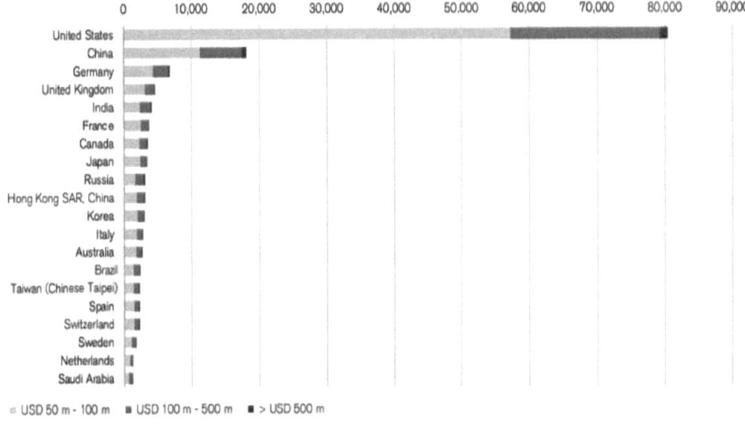

Source: James Davies, Rodrigo Lluberas and Anthony Shorrocks, Global wealth databook 2019

The share of total global wealth held by the U.S. is 29%.[51]

---

[50] Credit Suisse: Global Wealth Data Book

[51] Credit Suisse: Global Wealth Data Book

GDP per Adult	Wealth per Adult	Total Wealth - $ Trillions	Share of World's Wealth
$ 85.30	$ 432.40	$ 106.00	29%

None of the other countries come even close to the U.S. share which is 29%.

The remaining question is by what means was it possible for the U.S. to gain such large wealth so rapidly? Did the relative reliability of the investments in U.S. equities act as the dominant attraction for most of the global wealth?

Rising Temperature as a Climate Threat

The greatest threat to mankind, as identified by the current World Economic Forum, comes from a changing climate. The global temperatures are rising. [52]

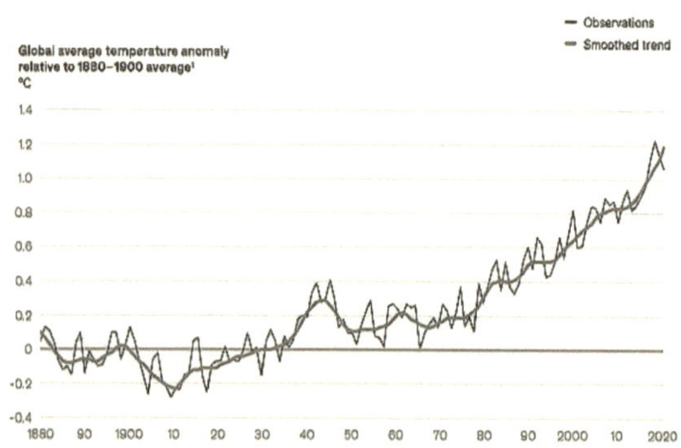

Rising temperatures will cause arctic ice to melt and coastal lands to flood. Despite denials, mostly from the U.S., there is no question about the

---

52

Climate%20risk%20and%20response%20Physical%20hazards%20and%20socioeconomic%20impact

s/MGI-Climate-risk-and-response-vF.ashx

rising threats to mankind from the weather. Coastal flooding of the most prosperous human towns, rising droughts of arable lands and choking temperatures are now accepted as scientific predictions.

Rising average temperatures do not simply mean balmier winters. Some regions will experience more extreme heat while others may cool slightly. Flooding, drought and intense summer heat could result. Violent storms and other extreme weather events could also result from the increased energy stored   in the atmosphere. One of the most serious impacts of climate change is how it will affect water resources around the world. Water is intimately tied to other resource and social issues such as food supply, health, industry, transportation and ecosystem integrity.

Increases in Temperature and Precipitation

The projected shifts of the climate are anticipated for 2030 and 2050. Material deteriorations are projected for China and Africa. [53]

---

[53]

Climate%20risk%20and%20response%20Physical%20hazards%20and%20socioeconomic%20impact s/MGI-Climate-risk-and-response-vF.ashx

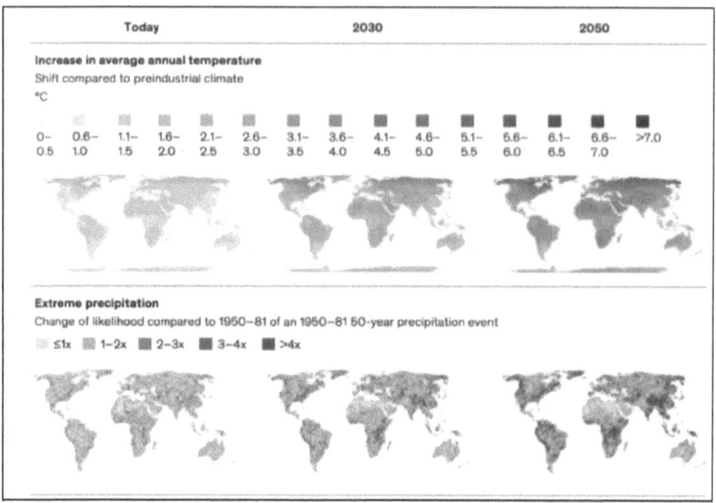

Elaborate maps have been now drawn by many institutes that are engaged in climate studies. The projected impacts of climate change are now starting to gain the shape of a likely reality.

At the recent meeting of the World Economic Forum the assessment of risks to the future of mankind concluded that the projected impacts of adverse climate will rank higher than all of the other risky scenarios.

Rising seas could affect three times more people by 2050 than previously thought, according to new research, threatening to all but erase some of the world's great coastal cities. New research shows that some 150 million people are now living on land that will be below the high-tide line by midcentury.

Asia Has Now 65%+ of the World's Population

This is one of the most critical indicators for setting the future of humanity. Exponential growth continues in Asia whereas North America, South America and Europe (declining) continue to keep only a 12% share of the world's population.[54]

---

54 Global Population by Region -HYDE

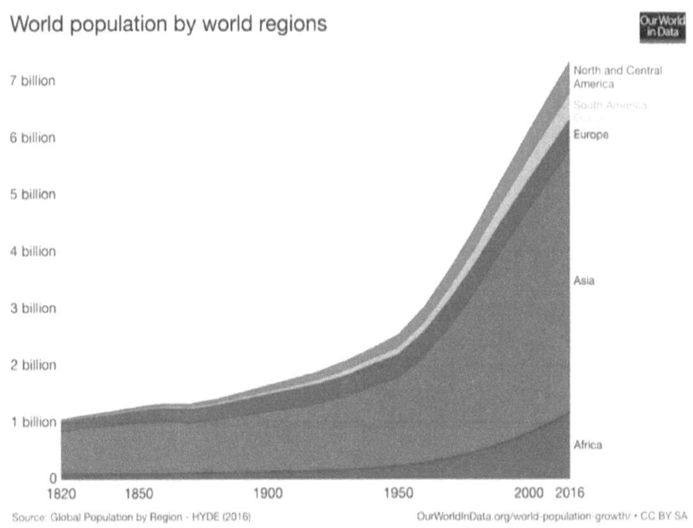

Population of Asia 4.4. billion, with China 1.4 and India 1. Population of Africa is 1.2 billion, Europe 0.7, North America 0.6 and South America 0.4,

Projections of future population growth constitute the most trustworthy statistical forecasts. Starting with a known headcount and then apply reliable birth rates a forecast of the projected mankind 20 to 50 can be established.

Declining birth rates and increased longevity in developed regions should be contrasted with explosive increases of population in Asia, which starts from a large base.

The relatively small contribution of Africa reflects low life expectancy despite a high birth rate.

Africa is Larger than USA, Europe plus China

The usual global maps tend to mislead about the size that can be attributed to Africa. [55]

In fact, the lands occupied by the USA, Western Europe and China can be placed on the map of Africa with land still remaining.

---

[55] https://www.mckinsey.com/mgi/our-research#

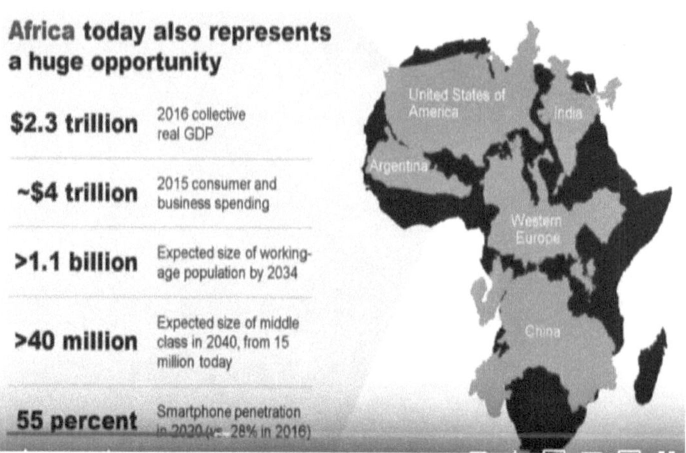

The enormous size of Africa needs to be better understood even though a large part of this continent is occupied by a desert.

Africa is recognized by scientists are the original homeland of mankind. Whether its inclusion as a consumer society can take place remains one of the principal tasks for world trade. Africa is the world's second largest and second-most populous continent, after Asia. At about 30.3 million km2 (11.7 million square miles) including adjacent islands, it covers 6% of Earth's total surface area and 20% of its land area. With 1.3 billion people as of 2018, it accounts for about 16% of the world's human population. The continent is surrounded by the Mediterranean Sea to the north, the Isthmus of Suez and the Red Sea to the northeast, the Indian Ocean to the southeast and the Atlantic Ocean to the west.

Asia Consumes 26% of Global Goods

The expansion of Asia's economies from a rising prosperity and supported by improved health care creates conditions for more than a half of the global consumer goods to be acquired by China and Asia. [56]

---

[56] https://www.mckinsey.com/mgi/our-research#0

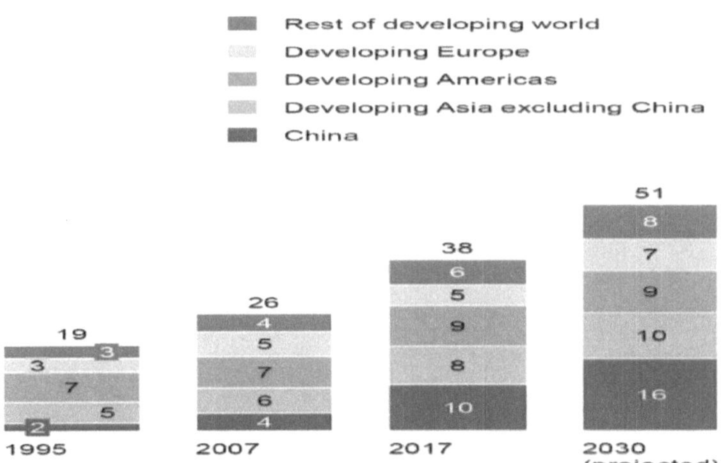

Weather the U.S. and the EU can capture a share of the rapidly growing consumer society is one of the principal challenges to viewing the future as a global society or as divided into two separate economies.

The projected 2030 consumption of consumer goods is $24 Trillion for less than 20% of the world's population (e.g. America $9 Trillion, EU $7 Trillion and $8 Trillion). Less than 70% of the world's population has a rapidly growing consumption of $26 Trillion.

Since 1945 the world has expanded largely under U.S. dominance, accruing most of the capital wealth to the U.S. Whether the emergence of a new and powerful power in Asia will leverage the accumulated U.S. capital for the benefit of a harmonious global society remains to be seen.

The future of the 21st century will be propelled by new technologies. It remains to be seen if technology will continue to be seen as a global possession.

Consumers Move from the U.S.

Until the turn of this century, population growth generated more than half of all global consumption. But between 2015 and 2030, three-quarters of global consumption growth will be driven by individuals spending more. This shift has profound implications. What's now important are emerging demographics that finds that nine groups will generate three-quarters of global urban consumption growth to 2030, and just three of these will generate half of consumption growth and have the power to reshape global consumer markets over the next 15 years.

The great missed opportunity for the USA is loss of participation in the rising Asian and African consumer market of 2.4 billion people. [57]

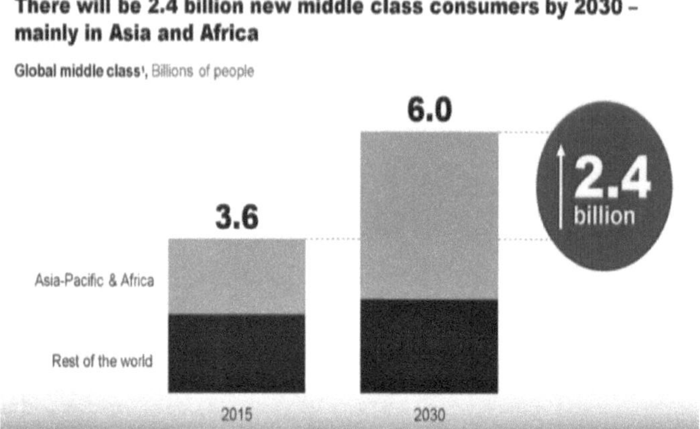

When tracking the evolution of the global economy we will concentrate on tracking the directions of global trade. Will the 2.4 billion new consumers by supplied largely from an international value chain, or will the political divisions create a bifurcated world?

The current indications indicate a separation of the world into two separate sectors, each with their own currency and technology supplied from local sources. It remains to be seen if such prophecy will actually materialize.

---

[57] https://www.mckinsey.com/mgi/our-research#0

Conclusions

Based on significant average incomes in New Canaan and in similar communities they should consider themselves as belonging to islands of privilege living in the peace of enclaves that can be described as "heaven". On a global scale this would include over a million residents now residing in communities such as Palm Springs, Maui, Zurich, Luxembourg, Taipei or Geneva. Of course, such estimates would apply only to the middle class and not to the minority of millionaires or to individuals living in poverty.

Our 2020 findings are:

Personal Conditions = OK

National Circumstances = Uncertain

Global Prospects = Yet Unknown

Author Biography

PAUL A. STRASSMANN's career since includes service as chief corporate information systems executive, vice-president of strategic planning, systems researcher and professor. He earned an engineering degree, a master's degree from MIT and a PhD from the George Mason University.

Strassmann joined Xerox as director of administration and information systems with worldwide responsibility for all computer activities. He served as the general manager of the Information Services Division with responsibility for corporate data centers, communication networks, administrative services, software development and management consulting.

In 1990 he was appointed to a newly created position of Director of Defense Information and member of the US Senior Executive Service, an appointment awarded to only 0.3% of DoD staff. Strassmann had policy oversight for Defense Department's information technology expenditures. He is the 1993 recipient of the Defense Medal for Distinguished Public Service - the Defense Department's highest civilian recognition, also awarded to four Presidents. In 2002 he was recalled as the Chief Information Officer of NASA, with responsibility for the computing information infrastructure. He received the NASA Exceptional Service Medal for his services. In 2000, he was cited by the Assistant Secretary of Defense for work as one of the executives responsible for advancing U.S. information capabilities.

Mr. Strassmann was Professor at the George Mason University and editor of the Armed Forces Communications & Electronics Association. He served as Chairman of the Board of Directors of Queralt and was leader of the InfoSecurity practice of the International Data Corporation.

He held appointments as Adjunct Professor at the U.S. Military Academy at West Point, Visiting Professor at the University of Connecticut, and Visiting Professor at the Imperial College, in London. His public roles included presentations to the US Senate, the US House of Representatives, the Board of Governors of the Federal Reserve, the British House of Commons, and the USSR Council of Ministers. Strassmann served on the Boards of Directors of Alinean, InSite One, McCabe Software, Meta Software, and Trio Security.

Strassmann is recipient of the Stefanik Medal as a guerilla commando from September 1944 through March 1945 in Czechoslovakia.

www.ingramcontent.com/pod-product-compliance
Lightning Source LLC
Chambersburg PA
CBHW051225250726
48655CB00006B/2594